SOME SKETCHY NOTES ON MATTER

By the same author:

The Future Un-Imagine (with Caren Florance) (2017)
The Told World (2014)
Thing&Unthing (2014)
Interference (chapbook) (2014)
Of Sky (chapbook) (2012)
Views of the Hudson (2009)
twelve labours (with Gwenn Tasker) (2009)
The Night Ladder (with Lisa Pullen) (2009)
Parts of Speech (2007) (winner of the Thomas Shapcott Prize)

SOME SKETCHY NOTES ON MATTER

ANGELA GARDNER

RECENT WORK PRESS

Some Sketchy Notes on Matter
Recent Work Press
Canberra, Australia

Copyright © Angela Gardner, 2020

ISBN: 9780648404248 (paperback)

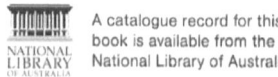
A catalogue record for this book is available from the National Library of Australia

All rights reserved. This book is copyright. Except for private study, research, criticism or reviews as permitted under the Copyright Act, no part of this book may be reproduced, stored in a retrieval system, or transmitted in any form by any means without prior written permission. Enquiries should be addressed to the publisher.

Cover design by Recent Work Press
Set by Recent Work Press

recentworkpress.com

'the line does not imitate what we see— rather, it 'makes us see'

Klee, 9 Objects and Things

Contents

Glass

Glass	3
Unkempt if you will	4
Waiting for the rain	5
The eye as passenger	6
I return to my body (I turn for home)	7
Clean eyes	10
Many ways, in pieces	11

Mapping progress

Battlefield photograph	15
The car stalled at Lawnton	16
Trees leaning down	17
Mapping progress: A pastoral (Contested Ground)	18
Reality very close to a dream	21
Early lessons in colonialism	23

Killing time

What can't be punished	27
Killing time	28

Notes to architects

1—Hotels	37
2—The private house	38
3—Shopping malls	39
4—Car showrooms	40
5—Piers	41
6—Towers	42
7—Bridges	43
8—Pleasure grounds	44
9—Demolition	45

In the valley

Misunderstanding	49
Three lessons from a market economy	50
Blankness	53
Roadblock of wants	54
In the valley	55
Oh yes we should	56
Not thinking about the circus at the circus	57
Some sketchy notes on matter	58
A tragedy in four hundred parts	61
Crossing the line	62
It, I said	63

Horizon

Our heads are full of cities	67
W rapt	68
Breath	69
Plenish after Paul Celan	70
Figures on Manly Beach, Anne Zahalka	71
Horizon	72

Glass

Glass

I lay down to enter the sky as birds will do
so openly, so traversable.
A blueness all around lifts above, chases the ever
-moving horizon. Not lining, not flap but somehow
dimensional. Further, further through the branches.
Exultant even in the slow progress of clouds.
Until the house is a sky made of uprights of forest
and everywhere the leaves are set against more leaves
in the trees and in the hanging of the clouds.

Unkempt if you will

mazy with grass seed and insects.
By which you read Summer.
A season warm and static. Nothing
surely can happen beyond the buzz
of the bees in the salvia. Stay here, lie
on the lawn the whole day
until its light and heat dissolve into night
until at last we must seek shelter.
Forget about the dog, unpredictable
on the boundary, the strange look
she gets in her eyes as she lunges,
hurls her longing and discontent
repeatedly against the fence.

Waiting for the rain

Restless. The wind a pressure, an equalisation come to heat
and violence. And the garden, just a hill-top field between
forest and more forest. Who could say it is an indulgence?
Elaboration of plumage concealed now at midday. Brush box
and red cedar, transiting down to the north to a stand
of blue gum, pine a boundary and wind-break to the west.
Turbulent paradise, thirsting. Only the bell-birds active
in their harvesting and destroying, and in that, insistent.
Their unremitting turbine, and behind that another turbine
of some greater force, and that only just held-back.

The eye as passenger

say blunt, say hone for distance and journey.
We miss, but this, this has edge, has axes
:the drift of conveyance. An eye runs along a surface forever
in transition, forever circling and dancing. Unfinished to finished,
the direction of shelter, a model of itself that faces its field
of possibility.
                    The eye as passenger on a back road, reaches
its not insubstantial fear (the too difficult/the nothing worth dark)
in the placement of a very large space. Absence as object
: background dissolved, foreground lost, no horizon but
our persistent engine, the shape of sound,
one thing substituted for another thing.

I return to my body (I turn for home)

       A bad day's work
:no animals, no equipment, no entertainment.
The vacuum cleaner vibrates, rattling its screws
a filthy heat pulsing from both ends. Turns out
we are merchandise, but by this point it's way past
time to pocket the wad of notes and move on.

       The body, the thing
we wake to each morning returns us from our nightly
avatars back into our bulky selves. Shape-shifted
and flying Ira is crumpled paper, Sheela is a soft toy
on a dark street. Morning comes, foot on a face,
climb the ship, the elephants, the disciples. The tower,
the stack, the fans. Whatever.

       Existence?
...well that's their orbit-swing around my head.
Crawl into a space without selfies.
And put me in the picture. How does that work?
The familiar room a one-way valve of unused volume.
In the corner Lily of the Valley dug up and dumped
in a plastic carrier bag.

       Human
amusing, and occasionally disgusting
pollutants upwell continually. It's a world of desire
:open your device, change this setting. Mouths
:soft things snag on hard things. CCTV
records the moment (but not the grief or rage
that follow).

                        And the aftermath?
Briefly moving on there is more moving on.
As a choice, it's an opening full of holes. Like using
oversize brown coveralls instead of indefinite pronouns.
Crisp-shirted at the beginning, wilting by the end.
That was the world: motes in the air, windows pegged
shut, the stuffing shaken out.

                            A garbage truck
moves along the road. Sun shines and disintegrates
(it can be gradual). There and not there. Between.
There is a sound of hammering, metal on metal,
bone on bone, flesh of chairs, the flaw in the mirror
that reflects only darkness.

                          Through the window
the sun, the rain, the wind. The gardens below
breathe a valley between buildings. The day's early
green accepts light as it falls, rain on the surface
of the world. Photons translate this as mobile phone
mast, apartment block, chestnut tree.

                                On the shelves
in the co-op there's butter full of fatty acids and
there's margarine full of emulsifiers.
Animal, synthetic, diglycerides and preservatives
visible pattern (iso-grid) stiffening.
My brain is shrinking through lack of sleep.

                                    Hold up.
Should we forgive large scale participatory actions?
Use insects as robots to soften the peculiar physics
of downward acceleration and resistance? It's not candy
-crush. Sheela and Ira return from the shop in time
for nothing to happen. Life goes on. Wasps deliver
their payloads.

There's a blurring
peak frequencies heavier than air, the changelog
with a fix for double tap. Embodied in digital
environments she went out without any money.
And we're the same: this happens, then that
happens. Cooling stacks. Surprise or confusion.
Dismissive lack.

It's fair to say
unwanted folds remain visible as a point of faith.
Selves or shelves? We are both small
countries/containers. Then someone asks "what
are the wasps for?" And we answer "Surely you know,
they are for themselves."

Clean eyes

The day is dull and turning to soft rain. Imagine
if I can find, oh the exact point where air stops
and this thing sky begins. The all-around of it I breathe.
When does it become the lacquer-hard sheen of troposphere?
What can it matter to trees that will slow the air to turbulence,
the changeable weather and mass they will captivate.
Words disappear in daylight as the daylight itself disappears.
If the sky listens it will learn it is lost. It's a question
of permissions of hidden contagion "Count the things,
don't worry what can't be counted". But I do.
That strangely human take on *purpose* that fits backlit lives
into plastic crates, that defoliates the *tidy* towns.

Many ways, in pieces

Watch the child until she goes through the door.
Do we learn: anything? That desire and light enter,
that we can choose analytics or ignore them.
It creates an economy in which we service each other
:the fire-tailed finch killed by ambition and certain clarity
the mouse drowned in a bucket and boiled for her bones.
Tundra defrosts in a methane stink of rot. Who thinks
of roses now? Really it's just a roll of the dice before
our armies invade or retreat into a forgotten region.
The many ways in pieces, made whole before
we reach gear ratio. Because it won't stop
it will just carry on differently and without us.

Mapping progress

Battlefield photograph

Into the meadow, our drifts of breath, seedheads sown, fog's reverent hush for recent history. A scratched and worn world the mind another limb. We must (leave) say goodbye, the idea of the divine battling salted skin and mouths of broken teeth for the hollows of our bodies.

While he *sleeps* each seed by its smell is sexual: coriander, basil, curls of calendula all now waiting. Imagine meeting under small flames, white-hot flowers in a mild degraded sky. To say so lightly *I am destroyed* when nothing that is said can make a difference.

The car stalled at Lawnton

The car stalled at Lawnton, she came to us immediately
having cradled the dying boy, passenger beside the road.
Morning just out of town along that stretch, memorial tinsel
in the summer sun and roses beside the trees. The talk
of weddings, children not invited, the costs of alcohol. Her own
sons at that point in the road, straight temptation high on some kind
of junk, where the cops set their speed traps under huge billboards
of grilled steak. Car lights wink beside concrete slabs
and formwork. Her flesh kept me. Everyone leaves, rewritten
first to last, the bright grass and the broken ditch beside.

Trees leaning down

Intelligence shines expectant in the sunshine: amoral, rain-soaked,
alive and intent. The *depths* of the forest
:built cities of insects, their paths through a blind underground
rise up before us swaying. Swarming hosts over light
and shade, chlorophyll doing its work. The exchange of water
and oxygen. The sky: permission to alter.

The trees lean down listening. Maybe not
but they lean down. If we took photographs we'd remember
:the scented sex canopy of flowers, fleshy slash of livid orange,
a shadow over (just a shadow), lichen discreet, the unfamiliar
(danger) out on the scent paths, a beetle as it falls unrighted
in the leaf-litter and struggles for its life.

That cleared horizon we design here at our backs,
gravity as it touches air, stones in the water. No
solitude the bees will hover. The ridiculous white cube we fill
with an idea.
The world goes about its business. How it all rises up before us
swaying, shelter of clouds tethered close.

I take myself to the edge of the water, shaded
but not from its music. We should respond - buried creature we cannot
recognise in spliced code, our probes reach in darkness and cold
to things we have made. If I leave every eye
will push against the wind, making
the air. Fireflies and rot, perfect imperfect, will resume again.

Mapping progress: A pastoral (Contested Ground)

Embedded in self, his head is his country, the bugles sound
in the rolling canopy. Now no question is comparable
to frequency, to exquisite belief

offered classically through *The Fallen*. Guns, in their blooming,
snatch insights, east of the slope is a mere rook sketch,
no natural forms, the land unshaped.

The map washes in things river-drunk until what was vertical fails
to hold, become spells of weather. Daylight all to rubble.
How will he know it is ended?

Currents, unsuccessful as the airy drowning and finely balanced
cumulus— the sky reduces fair buildings and birds flying away
to meaningless air streams.

And of spring, of snowdrops where production clutches the meadow
valleys - to demonstrate this, empirically,
prompts pilgrimage.

While our Lady of Isoclines, inherited from civic paternalism has clear
prospect over a whole firmament of visibility, advantage,
and iron-ore production,

between leaves, a wreath. No attentive observer in middle output
of resources replaces agricultural distribution with tonne kilometers
that is not "concurring."

A tradition of its utilization remains: coal mining some way before Forest.
Even as "hunting grounds" popularise road-pattern, until
Livestock believe in the land

and other, more interior, woodlands. Ship red cedar as balustrade,
to balcony forest industry, and its scenery of cyclonic depression,
enables water

more wayside shrine than system. Hachuring every outpost of every
village he struggles for the edge of the forest. Makers of one
and two-point perspective

see light on water, night's descent from the rich forest
floor of memory and history - and the vital Tree
of bent bough causes

conventional crosses and wooden saints to spontaneously bloom
in welded grapples and tracked loaders: the represented and
the represented side by side,

Enter better written weather integrals as weapons of war. A woods
-man's honour of rainfall, its surplus and pleasure, now ironically
becoming our *civil* timber.

The day is narrowing a confined foreground of the exhausted.
No choice comes clearly to mind, he is afraid for the reality
behind a reality he sees.

Propagandists of careless climatology disperse two thousand
mature, if captive, arrows and regimental frogging
into the gradient profile of rain.

The maps also acknowledge men died, their throats cut as examples
of the mechanical, with stipples so predictable
for Empire [to be] insulted.

The god lies deviated *poet-soldier-courtier*, the great river virtually
identical, devout of fertility, awaiting either mortality
or population replacement

while another hand clacks quoll or possum into twenty-six editions,
to the very epoch of nostalgic groves, allegorical in themselves
even without the *pissing putti*.

Here on the escarpment densely embroidered fronds manage exactly
the scale of gradients. A hog, in a gully two years already,
is duly noted, to be reclassified later by foresters.

The swamp holds each 'soldier's issue Poet's reconnaissance
map' : useless even as overlaid against contour-scale or
inclining toward return.

Works of the acclimatization (else: ash, aspen: the long poem) mingle
with the writings of war poets, dog-eared and collapsed
under the shade of the choropleth.

The hydrological divide presses on busily, creeks run at Forest's
edge; only the soldiers, detained, are to endlessly repeat
the parade ground marches of Empire.

He has reached his limits: of capability, of objectives, the control
of fuel. There is that feeling of not being in rightful place
or of a day that is too transparent.

Spruce and fir stand raptly out of place as either side balances
up where it's hot on the ridge, in country that straddles
a line's standard thickness.

Reality very close to a dream

I know it can be played two ways—the irony thing
: straight down the line or as an idyll, not a cascade of defects.
We are all other and curious and scattered;
enticed by the language of difference or inflorescence.

Ultimately it's about family: one brother in a cupboard,
another in a hole in the ground. And how one summer's day
bees flew in a window seeking their robbed honey and the flowers
strewn on a bed in the early morning.

During this time my brothers were themselves constant
collision-events, ready to engineer any earthquake between them
or any who stood in their way. A bit like the genius in sling-backs
the younger lad had a charm for stillness.

We keep faith, keep visiting their difference: one who lives
under power lines, the other whose table is visited by hawks.
Other birds retreat when the sky descends to the earth
as befits the arrival of hooked beak and flesh-eating majesty.

As a child a piece of the youngest lad was removed; animals
sense this and follow him. Contrast this with the shallow horror
of the 24 hour news cycle that turns again the Voyeur's card
(a burning tower), its dreadful message of disruptive change.

For all of us there's always something missing.
One brother eats meat pies and Sunday roasts, the other—
Look it's an old story and of course you can see where it is going
:the uneven distribution of love.

Depending on who is listening we're each of us helpless.
We stand in need and the price is often too high. What I'm telling you

is all true, even though it came to me in a dream. For myself
I attempt the dialogue of the fold, the origami in the volta of a sonnet.

And I haven't told you of my sister who still dances
with mops and brooms, this long after she married her goldminer.
It comes down to all of our differing world views: for one brother
it's all politics, albeit as spectator; for the other it's a way of life.

We can see it in the holding on, or in the giving away,
or in the curating of a type of wealth. Me? I'm just trying to get by,
but for my sister it's something instructive. Refusing yields two
or more messages, takes many directions, lands us in different places.

And then there are different interpretations of wealth itself.
After a time you see it as coming from somewhere in the past
:gramophones or silver-ware. The argument in the hallway
where money was crumpled and thrown as a gauntlet.

I remember ritual visits to the houses of the old,
on one hand buns and bus-rides, processions of animals (as I believe
I said before); on the other strict injunctions to neither exist
nor betray any liveliness.   So this divide is not surprising.

In our family we don't even have to go back very far; only, in fact,
to the unfortunate incident after the wreck of the *Mignonette*.
Now when I look back I can see
the brothers never were each other's keeper.

Early lessons in colonialism

In the background in the hours to lift-off, the orbit, the undocking
we had our board game: with rich prizes to be handed to the victors.
All that week we'd counted down, said things when tv, when the world
was black and white and Nixon was bravado and fear and alone. Though
already it is true we'd seen burning children running down the road.
But today I cheerfully expanded my territories in a land grab
for the American mainland (via Kamchatka). A continent I could see
from my Russian window that was ripe for the picking
(we were war-gaming in a holiday house in Wales, in July 1969).

                              One brother held the whole of Africa,
the other bided his time in troop build-ups on the borders of Indonesia
(Australia having fallen to the youngest brother's control). My sister
was saying it wasn't fair and of course she was right but that was far
from the point. Which was? Unofficial alliances and getting game
-over, before the holiday was done. She'd be eliminated soon enough
but her tired cries and moans of protest weren't likely to stop.

                                        Unrecognised
in the fault-lines or the realities of history, our strategy depended
on probabilities and advantage and we thought of nothing else.
Large scale armies were represented by stained and polished
wooden counters. Losing nations, coveted for their riches, handed
to the victors. It was all logistics and ordinance. No talk of soft targets
or asymmetrical warfare, no talk of collateral damage. Not a hint
of massacre sites close to home, or how warfare is conducted now
:drone sensor operators, isolated thousands of kilometres distant
from their actions, manipulating the lives of mere shadow puppets.

I can piece together parts in the dark (just the mouth) and no voice
while we rolled the red and white dice, that would attack and defend,
and conquer the world. The moon gleamed, a pearl of great price

the thought of Apollo overhead adorning the heavens, her crew circling the costly and arid territory. Sometime in that long night, between the difficulty of keeping control of Asia and the inevitable fall of Europe before bedtime, we witnessed a first act of possession, bloodless and symbolic. Though what I remember was a bulky white suited man climb down a ladder onto a grey powdery *terra nullius*, the obviously lifeless earth's moon, to plant a flag. His reflective visor hiding sight of his eyes.

Killing time

What can't be punished

In my mind you stand in the doorway calmly raising your arm
sighting your handgun, lifting its barrel. You breathe out, and in
its pause, gently between breaths, at the still point, squeeze the trigger.

When everything black or white streams into our early evening
you are there, pixelated and slightly slurred, your nipple turned blue.
Briefly a bird sings, silence, then again it sings, no sound attaches.

The body, an enemy to itself, empties out. We punish what can't be
punished: we beat it and it learns nothing but those watching, watch.
Light coming from one direction. Looking takes away and gives. It is

precise (sometimes). Let me look away. We pass sunshine or it
surpasses us. A different mode aiming for what we cannot reach.
You, in the doorway, gun-sighted along the corridor.

Killing time
(A contract killer remembers America)

I

The snow-lodge in Vail? No, never got an invite.

Sometimes I'd go to Roberto's condo in the Keys, stand at the window
for its heady views. Rumour was he paid for it in cash.
Mostly it stood empty. He'd wait for rough weather to stay over.
Mornings, after a storm, he'd head out alone to beachcomb
for the King's Crown Conch, Lace Murex, the Alphabet Cones.
I'd slip past the doorman, through the marble foyer under gold
and crystal chandeliers, where Columbian drug-lords in vicuna coats
chatted at the elevator. Upstairs we'd admire his shell collection
laid out under the glass in specimen tables.

The main, family house was in Coral Gables.
I'd drive through its border gates, slow down for its tree-lined
avenues, automated sprinklers, driveways of RVs and European cars.
The *abuela* would smile to my 'encantada de conocerlo'
before returning to the kitchen, and we'd talk of politics
the children, the coming vacation.

Me? I stayed in a crumbling Deco hotel on Miami Beach.
Lunch stop at Wolfies for lox, avoid the sweet Jewish bread.
God, even the cigars tasted of sugar. All the snowbirds lined up
on stoops and anyone who could still walk, the entertainment.
Streets of auto-repair shops, takeout windows selling
paper cones of Cuban coffee, cafés selling black beans and rice.
(Young women: if you want to avoid the hisses of young men
in their long wheel-base cars, pumping music and testosterone
walk the opposite way on the sidewalk, so they can't curb crawl beside you).

One down. Warm nights, everyone out on the streets. I'd take
the shortcut at the off-ramp. If I missed the traffic signals, old vets
would push their chairs and amputated limbs against the hire-car
its implicit invite to minor collision, to tempt an open door,
the keys dangling ready.

II

Kelly's family were magicians from Sydney.
She met Jeb on holiday in America. It was after he got back
from Costa Rica and all the trouble he'd been in there. Just a low level
drug-runner, sure, the patch over one eye looked good but
it was from a childhood game of bows and arrows gone badly wrong.

Kelly settled down, small clapboard house, him in the yard business
him his own man. Summer holidays at the family lake-house
water skiing, eating watermelon in the shallows, those stupid
seed spitting competitions. Back in Gainesville, and a job to do.
Eugene, Jeb's Dad, would come by in the patrol car,
ease his gun in its holster off onto the coffee table and hold out
his arms for the toddler.

Shoulda known when the driver rested a handgun on the dash
that things weren't going to go easy. I was the decoy there
to keep Jeb occupied. Whatever he suggested I was up for:
Tequila Sunrise as a breakfast wake-up? What? Oh sure.
Drink while you drive Jeb? Sure.
Red hot chilli pepper laid with the cutlery? Sure how hot can they be?
Feed the alligators in the swamp at night? Sure Jeb, sure
whatever you say.

Marshmallows don't travel far from the hand when you throw them.
Cast the flashlight beam out into the swamp and their red eyes
are already on their way for you.

He was old school Floridan, Confederate, white-boy
and everyone was under suspicion. Kelly and the kids holed up in the house
a posse of pit-bulls roaming the yard between her and the gate.

As I said, Kelly's family were magicians from Sydney
:children's parties mostly, conjuring rabbits out of hats, gold coins
from behind ears, 'Find the Lady'.

We caught the early morning flight, one of those tin-can planes
where you can see right through the windshield from your seat. The tower
giving permission to leave, the runway ahead, then that magical moment
when the plane lurches up into the sky and away.

III

Flew into Denver (another time, different job). Mile High. Base camp.
The grand staircase of the downtown hotel felt like an assault on Everest.
Next day I picked up a hire-car and drove up higher, into the Rockies
west beside the Silver Plume then south onto the 91 at Copper Mountain,
with that resiny scent of the pine forests drifting through the windows.
It was so inviting I had to pull over to a recreation area, sit beside
a sparkling stream. The hiking trails led off into the trees
but it was hunting season and so no way was I going to let some cowboy
amateur with a new shotgun use me for target practice.

Near Leadville the 91 meets the 24 through to Buena Vista.
Up here the air is thin and hot and dry. We were headed to a ranch
in the flat of the valley under the Sangre de Cristo mountains.
That night we talked around the campfire, coyotes howling behind us
and the moon hung over the mountains like a lantern.

San Antonio you cross into Neuva Mexico but even before then
the towns have Spanish names. Just before Taos,
the Rio Grande cuts through a deep ravine. Out on the steel span bridge
the sun beat down hard on us and the wind pushed even harder.

We pushed back. It's about 800 feet down there to the river.
As I said to Roberto later: it's a useful thing to know.

Anyway Tiwa people of the Santa Clara Pueblo met their first incomers
in 1541, in the men of the Vásquez de Coronado expeditionary force.
The land was Tiwa; then people said it was Spanish; then they were told
Mexican (back when Texas was briefly its own nation around 1836);
then American; now it's back being Tiwa. Which if you ask me, they knew
all along. The Feast Days gained the names of saints, that's all
:San Lorenzo, Santo Domingo, Santa Clara, and the deer and buffalo dances,
if not the deer and buffalo themselves, continued as before.

We arrived early but the Corn Dance had already started. After I grabbed
fry bread and coffee from a stall in the car park I went to stand
among the adobe houses in the square. Here the dignitaries
sit on those stackable plastic chairs up near the front. The Corn Festival
is slow work under the Summer sun.
Young women do a stomp dance so that the heavy silver shells
sewn to their soft buckskin boots made a shimmering sound
over the beat of the drums.

After a while and the business done. I went to the stalls beyond the dancers.
More fry bread, some potters and a jeweller. This is what I wanted
to tell you about. When I walked over two Tiwa men were talking
about a blue lake up in through the forest in the hills. They broke off
when I arrived wouldn't say no more. I looked at the silver arrows
broken like replicas of those that come off the battlefields.

A dancer stood beside me, she was looking too. After a bit she picked
something out. As she stretched her silver shells rustled. The pendant
was fashioned like a ring-pull you get on a coke can. I stood a while longer
before reaching for a Zuni fetish. It's made of chrysoprase. You know,
that beautiful pale green crystal. The more impurities the stronger the colour.
And it was shaped like a horse with those subtle variations that means
it's the real thing, capable of bringing prosperity and success.

IV

The car ahead slid down the Shoreline Highway toward San Francisco
with me on its tail. It's a scenic route, curves and swerves for miles
between sheer rock wall and ravines and cliffs. Look down and the Pacific
reflects the last of the sunset in your eyes. It's a difficult road, doesn't take much
:a loss of attention, a nudge from behind, and he was screaming
to the seagulls all the way to the rocks below.

There's an auto graveyard not far from the Mission District where they'll crush
your unwanted car real quick (they say to save on space). I walked from there
on streets so dark, so alone under a bridge that you listen for footsteps
coming up behind.

I was heading to a *taqueria* I like, up near 25th, serves tacos old style
:no rice, plenty of hot sauce and cilantro. From there, by bus. I
didn't need some young vandalising punk, brave with the spray can
daring me to do something. Could have been graceful but the knife
concealed in his jacket made him awkward. Didn't need the attention
stared out the window keeping his reflection in the corner of my eye.

Friends met me at a bar we know in the Castro run by two old queens
reliable and bitchy. Night turned to the first of day, all our cash
in one last pile of coins crashed down onto the bar with a laugh
and one of us (don't remember who) said 'give us a jug of something,'
like tequila could at least be absolution under that great flapping flag.

V

And here I was. No-one to meet. Nothing to do. That job in Chicago
it fell through: one side or the other sometimes has a change of heart.
Out the window the Mid-West is a series of circles in different colours
:bright yellow of rape, paler corn, then vivid green of who knows what
irrigated with water taken from the Missouri, the Platte, the Mississippi.
City of skyscrapers, city of railyards and beef cattle.

The Art Institute, strange buildings in a glass box, had displays of arms
and armour. A history of warfare. I recommend it. On the streets
the homeless, polite and helpful. Or you can take the el
out into the suburbs, to Oak Park where Frank Lloyd Wright
practised architecture and infidelity and then abandoned
both the horizontals of the Prairie and his wife for the verticals
of the office tower.

But there's a lesson in those swanky skyscrapers you see from the river.
Trump Tower with 92 floors of glass that changes colour from blue
to grey so prettily as light hits its stainless steel fins. The underused plaza,
a reminder of his reneged on promises of amenities and entertainment.
Worthless wasted and unusable, that's what his attorney said of the bottom floors
of empty retail that altered his tax assessment. Saved him money but someone
always has to pay the price so that fell to the rest of Chicago. Yeah,
I didn't know what I was doing there but the visit turned out instructive.

VI

No point telling you about New York City. I've told you about that before.
You've been there, I've been there. You can buy hot dogs there right?
New Orleans before Katrina? Now that was something. Okay it was busy
and thriving and happy, at least that's what the tourists saw
: Mississippi riverboats, beignet, blackened fish, Southern Comfort.

I drove the Manchac Swamp trestle. It's like you're walking on water
for near on thirty-seven miles. This was early in the year,
dogwood and magnolia a flowering edge, a wreath along the bayou.
No-one around. Ten thousand square miles of quiet.
One lone alligator sunning himself but more out of sight
the boat drifting beside empty fishing shacks, the engine killed
the water, silent, gracious in receiving its gifts.

For some reason this puts me in mind of the cemetery there in New Orleans.
The Saint Louis Number One. How they bury their folk above ground.

The force of water, not anything Divine. The whole city below the water table, so pumps go day and night. And how in those stories, before they worked it out, the bodies pushed up from their graves like it was Judgement Day.

Notes to architects

Architecture, of all the arts, is the one which acts the most slowly, but the most surely, on the soul

Ernest Dimnet, *What we Live By* (1932) pt. 2 chap. 12

1—Hotels

Hotels must accommodate, the almost alone. Curved hours of meeting, late not leaving, and trembling bursts of singing. Windows should overlook, not distance, nor too-close walls but the voices we give inanimate objects, cameras that comfort entranceways, and then catch all our unintended compositions in grainy narratives. Shall we enter these rooms as certainties we no longer believe, but behind a wash of air-conditioned conversation, leave as an unintelligible hush of dimmed light? Remember this is rented space, not just for the business of sex or gambling, so balconies need only be momentarily giddy. Money should instead be spent on the loneliness of carparks, impressive foyers, staff that will not disturb carpeted silence. In the bar always the same two clients, existing in the almost visible, almost accessed half-life—the self in empty corridors.

2—The private house

It is not surprising that some may turn to Brutalism, but on steep inclines it can never compete with bright metal. Why not think of demolition and self-build by androids rather than the versant psyche? Let large boring machines provide an in-detail look at how we choose to live. Exposed heretics upscale Rachmaninoff's ten preludes and fill a room more successfully than formal furniture, though freeing delicate wasps to inhabit overtired rooms may create interest. Are we coincidental with possessions? Could we know that for a shroud or a strait-jacket when it is the sky, motionless and unconnected, that closes in? I can't help excavate the foundations of such morality, but with wallpaper flashcards, lesson plans, worksheets, we may just teach a house to become a home again.

3—Shopping malls

These desiring machines should be entered dumbstruck until all unbearable needs conceal behind sheet glass. Design to contain, to trammel, and to control. Imprison at eye-level in static terror close by needful shiny wares that shove against each other humiliated and pursued. Our Age's grand architecture, greater than human scale! Lower ground this reduces all preferability to degrees of pleasantness still disconnected and made for landfill. These are silos of heavy responsibility that are purposed to enclose, to suspend, and by time and blank facade provide us walls of disbelief. And while we broil in fat suits, sulky and impatient, to feast on pallid chicken we'll know by our daily foot traffic, trekking through the gross and leasable areas, where people are spent.

4—Car showrooms

While the dollar drops buy anime but discard other therapy.
Choose instant retrieval at nightclubs and find luxury in the
sea's discreet emotional toll as it sweeps into well-lit atria
or navigates forests of kelp, dense with the latest song titles.
Between dysfunction and happiness are sex machines so big
their interior space can completely fill these sparkling reefs.
Those entering mustn't realise their worthless flush of skin,
or discern that it is chrome polished to its own quickness;
but be amazed by distance, carefree moments of hardcore
whimsy that will show places in seawater to dive for trinkets.
Where we are is but an aspect of time, as if the mind ready
for release is happening before our past, after our future.
Use the rule of unintended consequences to not turn away,
to not turn back: for love maybe, not for human propulsion.

5—Piers

Contemplate consoling, without poverty, the ocean's flow;
the return of a ship to its chain of stars within the liquid sky:
it is a challenge to in-sea building of tangential apparitions
the continuous and undirected movement that washes over.
Novelty sheeting such as sequins should adorn your pier so
at night, in starlight thus festooned, it emanates fragile epilepsy.
Will it walk on water or promenade gently under a weak sun?
Raised walkways depend upon their shape to float or sink
so choose Euclidean figures for firm but lightweight geometry.
Finally to these foundations of difficulty attach a spiny handrail
and landing stage for the rapid exchange of each sweet vice.
The question to ask is—how this structure, so seemingly male,
so hopeful in its quest, wears undergarments of lacy ironwork
so visible and proud, that say—why fix when you can float?

6—Towers

This isn't glass or steel we make, but captured sun and
cloud, fastened only with such impossible ideas as built
the towering air itself. While birds will test its heights
have we allowed for music and emotion that may surge
at windows in gusts of light that fill with flapping sky?
Then weld whole blocks of cloud, water or gases into arcs
to resist these high winds in all their unreality. They are
gods - unruly, thunderous, beautiful, and insensitive.
Your roof should forgo both antennae and satellite dish,
instead install a tuning fork of a delicious tonic hum,
to form sky pagodas inside each worker's puzzled head.
The sky is molten, sheer and un-climbable, so lose your
self, lose sight and overreach, for what could we see
from these heights? Who could we be at these heights?

7—Bridges

... And so to build a bridge that is interpreted from stones
that are smooth as birds' eggs, with its many arches thin
shelled in glass fibre concrete. It should be self-anchored
and knowable, and never once delimited by its function.
The dimensions of it are deep and difficult to calculate;
the approach to it a long and curving anticipation, so that
the lights upon its far shore may mimic migrating geese.
Under construction, it could resemble psychology,
as much as steel, to cope with the unequal pressure.
Let it underpass or overpass as required. And although
you'll improvise upon the builder's central piers ability
to carry us over obstacles; it will be our own imperative
to leap cleanly over spaces, that will, by clever thievery,
show us a width of sky below its span.

8—Pleasure grounds

Let us speak pleasingly of affinities and a place of pleasure
where brief doves wash full stops from many hours of repose
and almost perfect cloud-grapple escapes the walls of reason.
Only yesterday the rush to know: for things to start at the end
and pleasure and beauty not to be such obvious beginnings.
Recall idleness. Question plenitude: windows and rainstorms,
our strict observance of a world that is now a store of wealth,
our pittance of crows, and stones, the tail ends of our journeys.
Quietus isn't an entry condition, so I wouldn't start from there:
instead use the steps of an escalator as they topple at the brink.
In some ways it is best to avoid the infinitive although you can
be guided by available materials such as milksops and honey.
You may include sundry domes and various other pleasantries
include a final scent: a lover's mind, our own...

9—Demolition

During dissolution, breakages, concrete rubble, corroded metal pipes or rusted wire, will trail unread onto the wrecked walls. We'll long to build our plinths not in tiles or vitreous enamel, but using shadows and malaise...in dark materials that require us to abandon the bright-coloured machinery of prior projects. To look instead for an imperfect backdrop to install our signs that must point to missing objects of no obvious purpose. Build silhouettes: of hoppers, wheeled cauldrons and trolleys that lack any opening to interpretation or to the story world. Through this state of grace withheld, they'll bring the ultimate excuse for paradox and the libretto of trucks. Precision objects that are from such decay reconstructed, cannot achieve posterity. Designate days of hardship, resist self mutilation's understorey —much can be made from indirect entropy and preformed lulls.

In the valley

Misunderstanding

                         A kind of lust forces us back
:the sky, the city, all a misunderstanding. See how pale it is
a different place each time, familiar yes but rearranged
as fear. The ride under our bodies kicks along. You are no longer
:disfigured in all the figuring and transfiguring. Mile upon mile
of the wrong beer, the wrong wine. It is all so heady!

                         The handsome young arrive
to rescue us and spruik God and the value of Business School.

           Is it any wonder our filtering organs choose this moment
to opt out with painkillers and ice-packs. Face and eyes drift into bottles,
arrange themselves on a shelf to observe this latest attempt to represent
the dark-star of Empire in texta pen.

Three lessons from a market economy

I. How to save money by buying

On the radio at waking
someone from London explains
it was the *Interbank* rate that was manipulated
—oh well, that's all right then, the economy
of Ancient Rome was fragile also

—not enough cash.

Before quantatitive easing
Suetonius wrote that the Roman general Vitellius
financed an entire military campaign
by selling just one of his mother's pearl earrings.
These things, so distasteful at the time,
are sometimes
necessary in order to get ahead.

I am all at sea
just like that tv show *Someone and Eva Cruise the Med*
(his name also with an E
seemed memorable until I tried
to remember it). With *Camilla Plots Against Kate*
I'm on firmer ground.
The Romans: Emperors, sisters, wives, mothers,
now they really knew how to plot.

Imagine the headlines if Agrippina, handy
with poisons, got hold of Diphacinone. But I digress,
back to the economy:
slaves were cheap and plentiful and the coinage
worth less than face value.

II. Easy ways to make money in rebounding industrial stocks

Suetonius, though scrupulously exact, took omens
seriously

Are the DAX are up or down?
The finance report most mornings is a good way
to start the day.

Back in the Ancient World, most trade was maritime:
grain from Egypt, tin from Cornwall, olive oil
from Spain.

        There was an incident where Julius Ceasar
was ransomed by pirates—hey we all know that feeling.
Light trading day, wind hardly in the sails, but
out to conquer the world and bam!

He took exception to the price on his head
tried to talk them up—and even now
cash continues to out-perform.

In the market a gentleman's word is his bond
so when he promised to crucify them he really meant it.
He wasn't talking
debt syndicates ascribing upside price action to short covering.
No, he was talking
nailing the bastards to a plank of wood and then some.

And he did. Word is my bond, standard punishment.
My bloody oath.

III. How to trade forex like a pro in under an hour

Remember when people used to collect bank-notes?
—a nice hobby for children, foreign travel
without the risk. ... my brother had a glass jar
filled with foreign coins.

Take the *as*, made of copper, could buy a pound of bread,
a litre of cheap wine
or *apparently* if you believe the graffiti
the services of a very cheap prostitute.

That would hit the news
even before forensic audits or corporate credit card fraud
very cheap does sound bad.
It's that move from theoretical to real
with consequences that could bite you in the as.

Suetonius again, this time about Julius Caesar:
who at a statue of Alexander the Great (in Spain)
fell to his knees weeping, jealous
that Alexander, at his age, had conquered the world.
That's what it's like in Forex
some young trader gets there before you and calls
his *high probability system*: informed decision-making.

But then young Julius was first
to put his living image on coins: a move designed
to put him right back on top.

Blankness

adrenaline (chemical wash) night through sirens
and residue, we recover the maimed in their stillness.
Bodies slump, akin to an exhaustion that is aftermath.
No mouth or eyes, and what was more, the torn heads
without power to communicate. An interruption then,
or possibly an intermission most urgent and pure.
Only afterwards I spy a shelf above. A line of cameras
looking back. Emptied, superseded (lens and shutter)
they are monstrous in our eyes (for we, by then,
had eyes to see).

Roadblock of wants

Witness into (then out of) after-image.
Hunts, full moon into (then out of) mouths.
Violence. The heart's frenzied climb
into searchlight on poison-baited hills.
How it costs. Lives made forensic
by their *reasonable* grounds (or not).
Stop and search. *Safer*, they say.
How it's not too early or too late
: how the streets expose *hold-up* men
and *do-nothings*. Expose what the stars
or we will bring.

In the valley

twilight
and tv there is no delay it is all echo. I shall fear
not for the lights are on in the bottlo, the money
off in deepwater, rearranged pixels, and retouched
talk. What's not to?

Beyond is shadow heresy, tidal breaths
a machine that inhales a thousand human silences.

Pop-up stores storm-front
past human-turnstiles, porn-star descriptors, public
humiliations, follow me home lights. And half-way
to splendour, hesitates in a doorway.

Mute it all:
the strange exhumed places we all mouse-click
where crimes are shallow graves, scraped and scab
-bed. Skin a pucker of stitches, a thread that pulls
flesh taut before it liquefies. In the Valley (of
gauzy bridal gowns), of body maintenance, the cheap
fluoro offers its own cold hard kiss, its plastic bags
of rotting gristle.

How to weld | what makes us
human | to our prosthetic needs.

Oh yes we should

oh yes we should listen up
of course we should | pleas
it is life and we are living

the empty click
on your pick-up. dumb
—found almost cuneiform pharma we use

and the weather just interrupts
the fragile carry of any old day of the week
you are right or game-over.

the pressure builds
is too immense until you climb the roof
| gleaming slightly | with a hammer

Not thinking about the circus at the circus

I am shiny, towing an absence of sound through a tunnel. Holding
wrappers of the world I've arranged with head dead and disengaged
as tumble and throw subside. High wire step through the empty ring
of the moon. Its four quarters quartered inside, arms strength,
arms grasp, spin, climb and fall.

                                A door slams, a body slams.
It's important to rebuff distraction. Self-violence works on the body
with near misses, forcing confidences to strangers: that gift
of unburdening. I listen: her in tangles of herself sometimes messy.
And it all looks fine to start with: doll-witted within a thing, within
an overbalance. It's an edge she licks, for its bloody taste, hidden
from any clean-up crew.
A hard surface, oh yes but then there is ballast that sweetens the acts
in icing sugar. Access is a problem. She knows he sees what he sees,
in a dismount, to kiss or breathe.

                            It all hangs on the tethered wrist
or ankle: The *idea of the real*, companion to that personal copy we each
separately hold. That interval between possible worlds, the hinge
it all hangs from.

Some sketchy notes on matter

Fade in, fade out. Scattering near misses on our way
to someplace complicated as cloud's fall. The earth
sunlit. On the river a current runs under
as people move things from 'place' to 'other'.
Let me carry that for you (it's a way of slowing
and looking).

I should have paid attention to fall speed
and the attraction of bodies. Laid violent claim
to shortcuts in the brain as they encode
and decode emotion with disruptive graphics.
But, hey, I didn't. There is a vector point in space
that has suddenly gone sketchy, the fabric not holding.

I'm not saying something is *like* something else.
It's more interesting to say it *is* itself and then actually
see it. Cement trucks line up in a new street; pump
suburb over mud. Land that's criss-crossed with creeks
and scrub. Reed banks, piled earth and muddy pools -
tangible interfaces with material properties.

Here is space to work in: vectors and colour-
saturation all on a sliding scale to desaturation.
Enough to shut out light mechanics. Human | Machine :
Machine | Human. We look up and turn the digital objects
over in our minds, render surface and associated sound
to an emotional density closer to self.

Information moves. (Send out the sentries!)
It can write every pixel value but predicts very little.
We've made an imperfect copy and the adrenalin
rush is fading. Across the surface, in non-planar

geometry, are unconscious events and high level
continuity that we feel could take some body weight.

In all this, *the world seems first hand*
any 'out of awareness' moment is closed: more and less.
Realities are simultaneous through the lens
and framed in the playout. It's affective behaviour
mediated by embedded neurotransmitters.
And how to tell one from the other?

Into this I see someone as they walk, feel
their consciousness, and the events that made it:
as superhero; as dwarf. Locate the neural switch
in the software of his brain, put him in an exoskeleton
see what pushes his buttons. Activate disgust, then
aversion: it's all chemical - one way or another.

His wife and child are gone from the funfair.
(Though I don't know how you could know this.)
In a culvert a child runs as if everything is still
the future. This is when we load all there is to know
of an earth engineered in its own darkness—calculus,
internal logic, the night sky, floodplains ...

The correlations are consistent and we've corrected
for terminal velocity and visible sightings. If
this is a dream then I am every character: values
intensified or changed to grey-scale. Hallucination
and delusion: funfair, parents, child all awash
with system-specified sensitivities and nonverbal cues.

Funfair, parents, child—you try to hold them
in your head because maybe (just maybe) it's the only
place they fully exist. And yet I need to free up
space in my life (not everything is held in the clouds).

Let's slow this down, do the calculations,
and see where the child is going.

Where is that child going?
We occupy verisimilitude or we occupy nothing but
proximate sticky coordinates. A simulacrum that moves
through landscape mapping probability, attention just ahead
of eye-track. Here we leave the road and are flying
without meta-analysis or magical boxes.

The buffers are always changing and *it is
unhelpful to think of this as poetry.* It's computerised
going nowhere junk. All those precise obligations
that look down while the sky piles up, house
on the edge of a cliff, (car) failing to start: it's all held
together with gaffer tape.

A tragedy in four hundred parts

On bright fields of water it was something to see
:rain filling the past, trees tall under cumulus.
What does it take to hold the sky in place?
The moving raft of sky a dark shadow of itself.
The miracle of it. All of us holding strings.

A crowd arrives to hand over hand it from the rooftop,
to set it in motion under our feet. Children jump
between clouds arranged like ice-floes.
An animal, another animal, hunter or hunted.
They chase in repetitions of superheroes
as if help will appear in mask and cape to call us all
in to bedtime.

                The crowd jostles now against the tug
of strings first in shock and then in pain. 'Put it back'
someone shouts 'Put it back' as the pushing and shoving begins.

Crossing the line

Retching below deck the endless hours across Biscay,
I don't understand the *undifferentiated* water, and that's
the truth. Not the deep: the fish that fly, not any of its
wonders or its terrors. And we're only part way through
simulating our new reality. Not through the source-code,
nor the updates. Not how it works: the plastic crap,
the whales, the carbon sink. You and I, we drew lots
to be here at the rails, to watch the half-way empty acres.
To be where the icebergs, that calve somewhere cold
and north of here, end up, streaming the eastern seaboard.
Less above water, it's their unseen icy bulk that disturbs
:how they surface in our dreams, blue and towering.

It, I said

Through the metropolis special glasses are required
directly, gaudy elastic and oversize socks. Possibilities chase
through a look from a window onto pale sky. Look
and somewhere it is. In tall houses and quiet, in company
a shelter (for morning). I arrive and it could be night,
(air-waves at a lake and a house). A desk anywhere writes.
How useful in recognising my own disturbance
its sonar pattern of *other*, limitations of the physical self.
The *what* of *What is there*. Your solid surface sends itself
back. Not introspective, going out into the world, finding.
Differences used to make a space in place of self.
A surprise because of distance and then we were close.

Horizon

Our heads are full of cities

See how I was. Happy in the shade
of trees! It springs up.

  In time   and weather

carbon-dioxide exhales.   An orchard
of damsons   and greengages

      and of bees.

I hold a photograph to show this   650 foot
of lumber   and meadow

    flowers waiting.

The busy venture: each worker with an
astrolabe   or fan

to beat the air before the daylight stars
of pollen. Our heads

are full of cities
exile of neon blocking light through light.

even so :how the moon revolves   around
the earth

showing her constant   inconstant
face   to heavens' daylight valves.

W rapt

things happen but not here
not where sun forgetting shines all day.
plastic-w rapt and joyous
a feast-day to the patron saint of | |

we already know how it will end,
another begetting—experimental
films shown in multi storey carparks
celluloid flapping, cars doing donuts
and a crowd that will reel around us
until we are giddy.

Breath

Ecstasy or invocation in the midst of battle
: balance, point of balance, movement and stillness.
What comes to the hand along a line of shadow
slow as breath.

                As when an archer reaches down
and where her foot touches ... a weapon.

And rising how the sky itself rises and falls
to meet her. Torso covered only by a black curtain
of rain, in a sudden swooning darkness.
Heartbeat then drone. The sound of temple drums.
Drumming. As if elephants breaking our ranks
are thundering, trumpeting, trampling.

Plenish
after Paul Celan

A swelling or blockage, the stopped trumpet
sounding imperfectly, broken with gold.
What of the voices in our ears? Listen.
The anvil, the hammer, and the stirrup
wait to be filled as each note lays itself down
inside us. And through the cracks
something molten, antiphonal, enters.
The cooled and planished surface a shape
and sound to ring from the bell foundry.

Figures on Manly Beach, Anne Zahalka
(after Nancy Kilgour), 2015

It has the stillness of *Un dimanche après-midi à l'Île de la Grande Jatte*, that recognisable indolence of a Summer day. Sun that warms our backs even as it dazzles headland cliffs with green alps, suggesting we lay down in the alternate violet-scumbled shade, here on the yellow zing of beach towel, the soft abutting lemon-wedge of sand. The figures, arranged, regard the sea (its arrested movement of the waves). A boy's semaphore-stance (looks straight to camera), a supplicant girl-child to her mother, a clothed man holds his surfboard, each we measure against the bright red beach umbrella with its furled tight flag. Sun dresses and boardies, bright towels and dark glasses, beach bags and bikinis, all the expected objects for a day at the beach. Receding: the sea and its successive blues, the figures and the bays, each a wave that day-long laps our moments.

Horizon

The feijoa flowers as if to itself. *All of this* (it
seems to say). *All of this.*
Out in the garden the lorikeets are reverent
in a chatty way. The light says we are beside the sea
a glimpse of water and fuschia.
There's kangaroo paw. In everyone's gardens
the horizon. We read
the possibility of summer in the sound of insects
the wind chilling, showers possible and changeable.
The trees wave their raggedy hands in the sky.
Every year pink blossom. Pollen drift in the air.

Afterword

Some Sketchy Notes on Matter came together slowly around preoccupations of safety and shelter at an individual, societal and global level. I also wanted to look at the tensions between digital and analogue reality, between the city and a natural world that exists without us, strange, compelling and precarious. At its worst these tensions become an imbalance, a violence, threatening not only the individual body but the entire planet.

The oldest poem in the collection is a sequence, 'Notes to Architects', offering humorous and probably spurious advice on built structures that promote neo-liberal strategies rather than human comfort. There are also long narrative poems that create a recognisable world of colonialism, capitalism and war, including that waged against the environment. Through an ordinary life (in the poem 'Killing Time' the ordinary life is that of an American contract killer) it is possible to see how living itself may work upon the soul.

At a formal level I use both sound and fractured word images as part of a distorting mirror between sensory input and interpretation. My mapmaking of human vulnerabilities, although necessarily provisional and incomplete, plots a journey from the profound problems that beset us to an awareness of our part in needless consumption and destruction. Just as architecture can influence lives, poetry can change how we see the world and our place in it, encouraging us to be open and fearless and take responsibility for our actions.

Notes

'Mapping progress: A pastoral (Contested Ground)' uses language appropriated from Simon Schama's *Landscape and Memory*.

'Some sketchy notes on matter' ... *the world seems first hand* from Katherine Coles 'Life: Studies in Fragments' quoted in turn from 'Life Studies' by Richard Coniff, NYT, February 2011.

'Notes to Architects' is for Amber Diaz Gardner

'Figures on Manly Beach, Anne Zahalka (after Nancy Kilgour), 2015 '*Un dimanche après-midi à l'Île de la Grande Jatte* - Georges Seurat 'A Sunday afternoon on the island of the La Grande Jatte', Oil on Canvas, 1884.

'Horizon' is for Sally, Richard, William and Isabelle.

An earlier version of *Some Sketchy Notes On Matter* was shortlisted for the *Dorothy Hewett Award for an Unpublished Manuscript* 2018

Acknowledgments

Antipodes (USA) 2016—The Car Stalled At Lawnton
Australian Poetry Anthology, 2018—A Tragedy In Four Hundred Parts
Australian Poetry Collaboration #24 October 2016—Figures On Manly Beach
Australian Poetry Journal 8.1, September 2018—Many Ways In Pieces
Best Australian Poetry 2017, Black Inc—Unkempt If You Will
Blackbox Manifold (UK) 2018—Notes To Architects
Cordite Poetry Review
    Transqueer Ed. Stuart Barnes And Quinn Eades, 2018—Roadblock Of Wants
    Land Ed James Stewart And Jane Gibian, 2017—Unkempt If You Will;
    Explode Ed. Dan Disney Nov 2016—Misunderstanding
Hecate Vol. 43 No. 1/2 2017 Periodical Issue Pg. 223-224—Early Lessons In Colonialism, I Return To My Body [I Turn For Home], W Rapt
The Long Poem (UK) 2018 Issue 19—Killing Time
Magma (UK) 2012 Issue # 54—Piers (From Notes To Architects)
Meanjin 2017—Horizon
Overland Issue #211 2013—Three Lessons From A Market Economy
Rabbit Poetry #24 2018—What Can't Be Punished
Rochford Street Review Issue# 19 2016—Not Thinking About The Circus At The Circus
Southerly 75.3 War & Peace Feb 2016—Battlefield Photograph
Styluslit March 2017—Plenish After Paul Celan
Tears In The Fence (UK) #67 Feb/Mar 2018—Trees Leaning Down, The Eye As Passenger, Clean Eyes
Tincture 19, 2017—A Tragedy In Four Hundred Parts
West Branch (USA) 2018—It, I Said
Yale Review (USA) 2020—Waiting For The Rain

Thanks as always to my first readers: G.C. Waldrep, Cherry Smyth, Laurie Duggan and Kerry Kilner. Thanks also to Caren Florance. Her artwork *Pleasure/Demolition* uses words from my 'Notes for Architects' series and to poet Owen Bullock for then singing my poetry in a public performance at *East Space Gallery* Canberra in March 2017. (*Pleasure/Demolition* was also selected for exhibition in the 2017 *Nonesuch Art Of Paper Awards* in Canada).

www.ingramcontent.com/pod-product-compliance
Lightning Source LLC
Chambersburg PA
CBHW032048290426
44110CB00012B/1006